EVENTS THAT CHANGED YOUR WORLD

AMERICAN COLONISTS SIGN THE DECLARATION OF INDEPENDENCE

by Marcia Amidon Lusted

PEBBLE
a capstone imprint

Published by Pebble, an imprint of Capstone
1710 Roe Crest Drive, North Mankato, Minnesota 56003
capstonepub.com

Library of Congress Cataloging-in-Publication Data
Names: Lüsted, Marcia Amidon, author.
Title: American colonists sign the Declaration of Independence / by Marcia Amidon Lusted.
Description: North Mankato, Minnesota : Published by Pebble, an imprint of Capstone, [2025] | Series: Events that changed your world | Audience: Ages 5 to 8 | Audience: Grades 2–3 | Summary: "The United States is a young country founded on complicated ideals—ones that it still strives to fulfill. Many of those ideals were established in the 1776 Declaration of Independence—when colonists decided to separate from Great Britain. With historical images and details about key events before and after the political separation, this book will help kids understand the impact of the declaration on the history of the United States. Uncover the details of events that changed your world in this Pebble Explore series"—Provided by publisher.
Identifiers: LCCN 2024006197 (print) | LCCN 2024006198 (ebook) | ISBN 9780756581152 (hardcover) | ISBN 9780756581466 (paperback) | ISBN 9780756581213 (pdf) | ISBN 9780756581473 (epub) | ISBN 9780756581480 (kindle edition)
Subjects: LCSH: United States. Declaration of Independence—Juvenile literature. | United States. Continental Congress—Juvenile literature. | United States—Politics and government—1775-1783—Juvenile literature.
Classification: LCC E221 .L928 2025 (print) | LCC E221 (ebook) | DDC 973.3/13—dc23/eng/20240307
LC record available at https://lccn.loc.gov/2024006197
LC ebook record available at https://lccn.loc.gov/2024006198

Editorial Credits
Editor: Ericka Smith; Designer: Terri Poburka; Media Researcher: Svetlana Zhurkin; Production Specialist: Katy LaVigne

Image Credits
Alamy: North Wind Picture Archives, 7, 18; Bridgeman Images: Peter Newark American Pictures, cover (bottom); Getty Images: Bettmann, 5, Hill Street Studios, 24, Hulton Archive, 9, 27, Hulton Archive/Keystone, 26, MPI, 10, 20; Library of Congress: 4, 15, 17, 19; Line of Battle Enterprise: 6, 12, 13; Newscom: Album/Prisma, 11; Shutterstock: Everett Collection, 23, FamVeld, cover (top), sirtravelalot, 25, Susan Law Cain, 21, wavebreakmedia, 28

Printed and bound in the USA. PO 5853

TABLE OF CONTENTS

Words in **bold** are in the glossary.

A Hot Summer Day

It was a hot summer day on August 2, 1776. Fifty men gathered in a room of the Pennsylvania State House in the city of Philadelphia. They were all members of the Second Continental Congress.

Pennsylvania State House

The men had decided that the 13 American **colonies** should separate from Great Britain. Everyone was quiet. What they were doing could cost them their lives. Each man signed his name on a **document**. It was the **Declaration** of Independence.

Unhappy Colonists

In 1776, King George III of Great Britain ruled the colonies. By that time, the British had passed laws and created **taxes** that angered the colonists. The king had also sent soldiers to the colonies to keep them under control.

King George III

Colonists protesting the Stamp Act

In 1765, the British passed the Stamp Act. Colonists had to pay a tax on items like legal documents, newspapers, and playing cards. Colonists protested and refused to pay it.

In 1773, colonists also grew tired of a tax on tea. A group went aboard a British ship in Boston, Massachusetts. They dumped boxes of tea into Boston Harbor. This would become known as the Boston Tea Party.

In 1774, the British passed four laws that the colonists called the Intolerable Acts. They were punishment for the colonists' resistance. One of the laws closed the Boston Harbor in response to the Boston Tea Party.

Boston Tea Party

First Continental Congress

In response to the Intolerable Acts, the colonists created the First Continental Congress. It was a group of men who represented 12 of the 13 colonies. The group tried to address problems with the British.

The group wanted the British to get rid of the Intolerable Acts. They threatened to **boycott** British goods and to stop **exporting** goods. They sent their list of problems to the king. When they were done, they planned to meet again the next year.

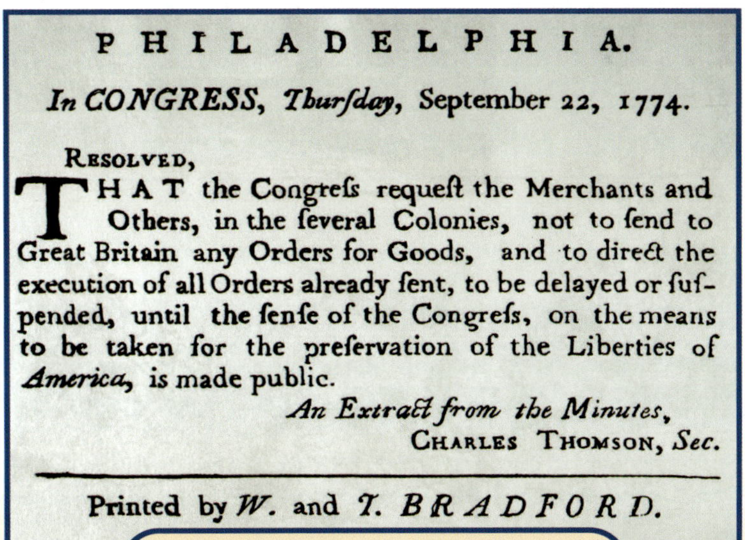

P H I L A D E L P H I A.

In CONGRESS, Thurſday, September 22, 1774.

RESOLVED,

THAT the Congreſs requeſt the Merchants and Others, in the ſeveral Colonies, not to ſend to Great Britain any Orders for Goods, and to direct the execution of all Orders already ſent, to be delayed or ſuſpended, until the ſenſe of the Congreſs, on the means to be taken for the preſervation of the Liberties of *America,* is made public.

An Extract from the Minutes,
CHARLES THOMSON, *Sec.*

Printed by *W.* and *T. BRADFORD.*

Order to end exports to Great Britain

The battle at Lexington, Massachusetts

But things grew worse over time. On April 18, 1775, British soldiers were sent to Concord, Massachusetts, to get the colonists' supply of weapons. The colonists found out they were coming. There was a battle the next day at Lexington, Massachusetts, and later at Concord. The colonists won at Concord.

More battles happened after the ones at Lexington and Concord. Two were in Boston.

George Washington (center) and the Continental Army

A Second Continental Congress met. The group created the Continental Army. George Washington was its leader. The American Revolution had begun.

Did You Know?

Paul Revere made his famous ride on April 18, 1775. He rode to warn the people who lived in Lexington that British soldiers were coming.

The Second Continental Congress also had to decide what to do about the conflict with the British. On June 7, 1776, Richard Henry Lee suggested declaring independence from Great Britain.

Some members of Congress were not sure about making this declaration. They would become **traitors** to Great Britain if they did. Others wanted a document that would tell the British why they wanted to be their own country.

Congress chose five members to work on the declaration. The group included John Adams, Benjamin Franklin, and Thomas Jefferson. They asked Jefferson to write the declaration.

Franklin, Adams, and Jefferson

Writing a Declaration

The writers of the declaration wanted it to say three things. It must say what they believed a good government is. It must tell King George III what was wrong about how he ruled the colonies. And it must tell Great Britain and the world that the colonies were free.

But the most important things that Jefferson wrote were "All men are created equal" and the government should get its power from the **consent** of its citizens.

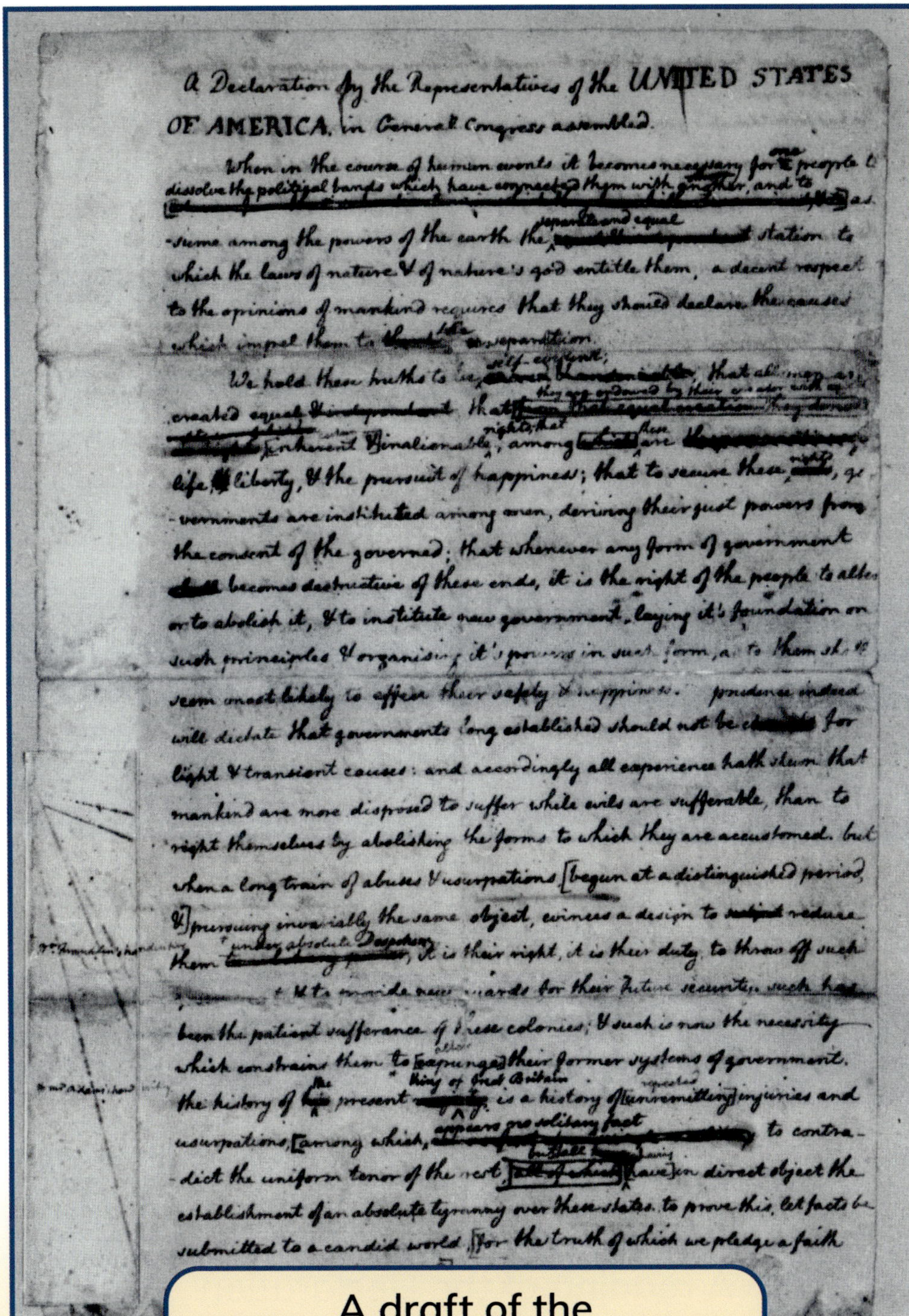

A Declaration by the Representatives of the UNITED STATES OF AMERICA, in General Congress assembled.

When in the course of human events it becomes necessary for the people to dissolve the political bands which have connected them with another, and to assume among the powers of the earth the separate and equal station to which the laws of nature & of nature's god entitle them, a decent respect to the opinions of mankind requires that they should declare the causes which impel them to the separation.

We hold these truths to be self-evident; that all men are created equal; that they are endowed by their creator with [certain] inherent & inalienable rights; that among these are life, liberty, & the pursuit of happiness; that to secure these rights, governments are instituted among men, deriving their just powers from the consent of the governed; that whenever any form of government becomes destructive of these ends, it is the right of the people to alter or to abolish it, & to institute new government, laying it's foundation on such principles & organising it's powers in such form, as to them shall seem most likely to effect their safety & happiness. prudence indeed will dictate that governments long established should not be changed for light & transient causes: and accordingly all experience hath shewn that mankind are more disposed to suffer while evils are sufferable, than to right themselves by abolishing the forms to which they are accustomed. but when a long train of abuses & usurpations [begun at a distinguished period &]pursuing invariably the same object, evinces a design to reduce them under absolute Despotism, it is their right, it is their duty, to throw off such government & to provide new guards for their future security. such has been the patient sufferance of these colonies; & such is now the necessity which constrains them to alter their former systems of government. the history of the present King of Great Britain is a history of repeated injuries and usurpations, [among which, appears no solitary fact to contradict the uniform tenor of the rest, but all have in direct object the establishment of an absolute tyranny over these states. to prove this, let facts be submitted to a candid world. [for the truth of which we pledge a faith

A draft of the Declaration of Independence

Their Declaration of Independence was **adopted** by Congress on July 4, 1776. It was printed so that everyone could read it. It was read out loud in cities like Philadelphia and Boston. And it was printed in newspapers all over the colonies.

A reading of the Declaration of Independence in Boston

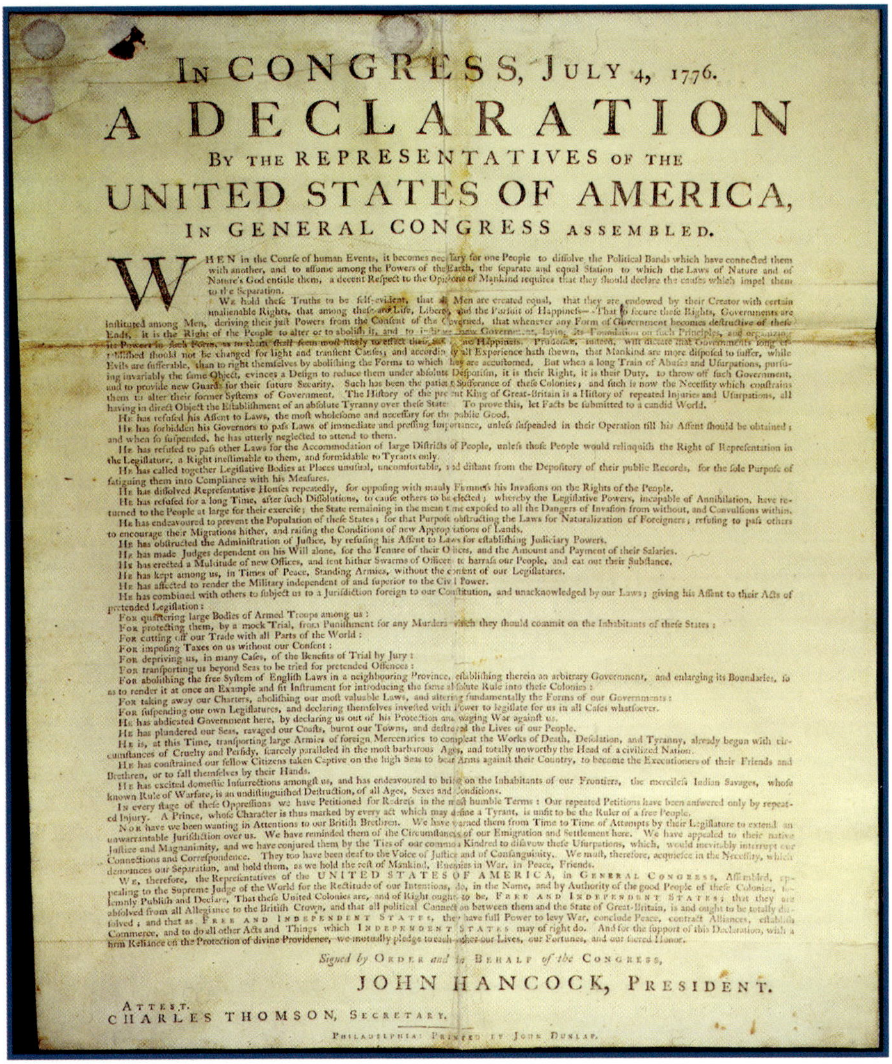
IN CONGRESS, JULY 4, 1776.

A DECLARATION

BY THE REPRESENTATIVES OF THE

UNITED STATES OF AMERICA,

IN GENERAL CONGRESS ASSEMBLED.

WHEN in the Course of human Events, it becomes necessary for one People to dissolve the Political Bands which have connected them with another, and to assume among the Powers of the Earth, the separate and equal Station to which the Laws of Nature and of Nature's God entitle them, a decent Respect to the Opinions of Mankind requires that they should declare the causes which impel them to the Separation.

WE hold these Truths to be self-evident, that all Men are created equal, that they are endowed by their Creator with certain unalienable Rights, that among these are Life, Liberty, and the Pursuit of Happiness—That to secure these Rights, Governments are instituted among Men, deriving their just Powers from the Consent of the Governed, that whenever any Form of Government becomes destructive of these Ends, it is the Right of the People to alter or to abolish it, and to institute new Government, laying its Foundation on such Principles, and organizing its Powers in such Form, as to them shall seem most likely to effect their Safety and Happiness. Prudence, indeed, will dictate that Governments long established should not be changed for light and transient Causes; and accordingly all Experience hath shewn, that Mankind are more disposed to suffer, while Evils are sufferable, than to right themselves by abolishing the Forms to which they are accustomed. But when a long Train of Abuses and Usurpations, pursuing invariably the same Object, evinces a Design to reduce them under absolute Despotism, it is their Right, it is their Duty, to throw off such Government, and to provide new Guards for their future Security. Such has been the patient Sufferance of these Colonies; and such is now the Necessity which constrains them to alter their former Systems of Government. The History of the present King of Great-Britain is a History of repeated Injuries and Usurpations, all having in direct Object the Establishment of an absolute Tyranny over these States. To prove this, let Facts be submitted to a candid World.

HE has refused his Assent to Laws, the most wholesome and necessary for the public Good.

HE has forbidden his Governors to pass Laws of immediate and pressing Importance, unless suspended in their Operation till his Assent should be obtained; and when so suspended, he has utterly neglected to attend to them.

HE has refused to pass other Laws for the Accommodation of large Districts of People, unless those People would relinquish the Right of Representation in the Legislature, a Right inestimable to them, and formidable to Tyrants only.

HE has called together Legislative Bodies at Places unusual, uncomfortable, and distant from the Depository of their public Records, for the sole Purpose of fatiguing them into Compliance with his Measures.

HE has dissolved Representative Houses repeatedly, for opposing with manly Firmness his Invasions on the Rights of the People.

HE has refused for a long Time, after such Dissolutions, to cause others to be elected; whereby the Legislative Powers, incapable of Annihilation, have returned to the People at large for their exercise; the State remaining in the mean time exposed to all the Dangers of Invasion from without, and Convulsions within.

HE has endeavoured to prevent the Population of these States; for that Purpose obstructing the Laws for Naturalization of Foreigners; refusing to pass others to encourage their Migrations hither, and raising the Conditions of new Appropriations of Lands.

HE has obstructed the Administration of Justice, by refusing his Assent to Laws for establishing Judiciary Powers.

HE has made Judges dependent on his Will alone, for the Tenure of their Offices, and the Amount and Payment of their Salaries.

HE has erected a Multitude of new Offices, and sent hither Swarms of Officers to harrass our People, and eat out their Substance.

HE has kept among us, in Times of Peace, Standing Armies, without the consent of our Legislatures.

HE has affected to render the Military independent of and superior to the Civil Power.

HE has combined with others to subject us to a Jurisdiction foreign to our Constitution, and unacknowledged by our Laws; giving his Assent to their Acts of pretended Legislation:

FOR quartering large Bodies of Armed Troops among us:

FOR protecting them, by a mock Trial, from Punishment for any Murders which they should commit on the Inhabitants of these States:

FOR cutting off our Trade with all Parts of the World:

FOR imposing Taxes on us without our Consent:

FOR depriving us, in many Cases, of the Benefits of Trial by Jury:

FOR transporting us beyond Seas to be tried for pretended Offences:

FOR abolishing the free System of English Laws in a neighbouring Province, establishing therein an arbitrary Government, and enlarging its Boundaries, so as to render it at once an Example and fit Instrument for introducing the same absolute Rule into these Colonies:

FOR taking away our Charters, abolishing our most valuable Laws, and altering fundamentally the Forms of our Governments:

FOR suspending our own Legislatures, and declaring themselves invested with Power to legislate for us in all Cases whatsoever.

HE has abdicated Government here, by declaring us out of his Protection and waging War against us.

HE has plundered our Seas, ravaged our Coasts, burnt our Towns, and destroyed the Lives of our People.

HE is, at this Time, transporting large Armies of foreign Mercenaries to compleat the Works of Death, Desolation, and Tyranny, already begun with circumstances of Cruelty and Perfidy, scarcely paralleled in the most barbarous Ages, and totally unworthy the Head of a civilized Nation.

HE has constrained our fellow Citizens taken Captive on the high Seas to bear Arms against their Country, to become the Executioners of their Friends and Brethren, or to fall themselves by their Hands.

HE has excited domestic Insurrections amongst us, and has endeavoured to bring on the Inhabitants of our Frontiers, the merciless Indian Savages, whose known Rule of Warfare, is an undistinguished Destruction, of all Ages, Sexes and Conditions.

IN every stage of these Oppressions we have Petitioned for Redress in the most humble Terms: Our repeated Petitions have been answered only by repeated Injury. A Prince, whose Character is thus marked by every act which may define a Tyrant, is unfit to be the Ruler of a free People.

NOR have we been wanting in Attentions to our British Brethren. We have warned them from Time to Time of Attempts by their Legislature to extend an unwarrantable Jurisdiction over us. We have reminded them of the Circumstances of our Emigration and Settlement here. We have appealed to their native Justice and Magnanimity, and we have conjured them by the Ties of our common Kindred to disavow these Usurpations, which, would inevitably interrupt our Connections and Correspondence. They too have been deaf to the Voice of Justice and of Consanguinity. We must, therefore, acquiesce in the Necessity, which denounces our Separation, and hold them, as we hold the rest of Mankind, Enemies in War, in Peace, Friends.

WE, therefore, the Representatives of the UNITED STATES OF AMERICA, in GENERAL CONGRESS, Assembled, appealing to the Supreme Judge of the World for the Rectitude of our Intentions, do, in the Name, and by Authority of the good People of these Colonies, solemnly Publish and Declare, That these United Colonies are, and of Right ought to be, FREE AND INDEPENDENT STATES; that they are absolved from all Allegiance to the British Crown, and that all political Connection between them and the State of Great-Britain, is and ought to be totally dissolved; and that as FREE AND INDEPENDENT STATES, they have full Power to levy War, conclude Peace, contract Alliances, establish Commerce, and to do all other Acts and Things which INDEPENDENT STATES may of right do. And for the support of this Declaration, with a firm Reliance on the Protection of divine Providence, we mutually pledge to each other our Lives, our Fortunes, and our sacred Honor.

Signed by ORDER *and in* BEHALF *of the* CONGRESS,

JOHN HANCOCK, PRESIDENT.

ATTEST.
CHARLES THOMSON, SECRETARY.

PHILADELPHIA: PRINTED BY JOHN DUNLAP.

Then, it was time for Congress to sign it. Signing their names was dangerous. They could be arrested as traitors. They could be put in jail or killed.

Hancock signing the Declaration of Independence

Congress had a copy of the Declaration of Independence written on **parchment**. This was the copy that Congress signed.

On August 2, 1776, about 50 members of the Second Continental Congress signed the Declaration of Independence. John Hancock was first. He was president of the Congress. He signed his name in big letters.

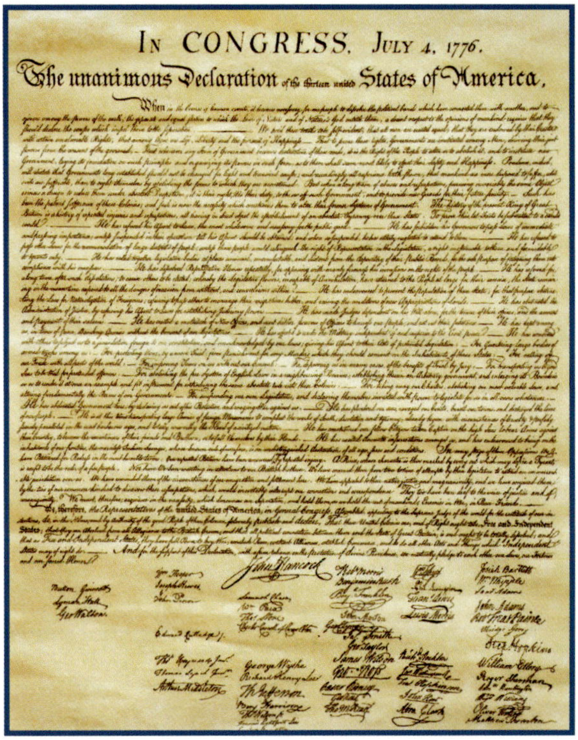
IN CONGRESS. JULY 4. 1776.

The unanimous Declaration of the thirteen united States of America,

By August 10, 1776, news of the Declaration of Independence reached London, England.

Did You Know?

Some people signed the Declaration of Independence after August 2. Eventually, it would have a total of 56 signatures. The last person to sign was Thomas McKean, after January 18, 1777.

Independence!

King George III found out about the Declaration of Independence. But he was determined to continue ruling the colonies. The American Revolution lasted until 1783, when the British and the colonists signed the Treaty of Paris. The colonists had won their independence.

The United States' Declaration of Independence created a new feeling of freedom in the world. It showed that people did not have to be ruled by unfair leaders.

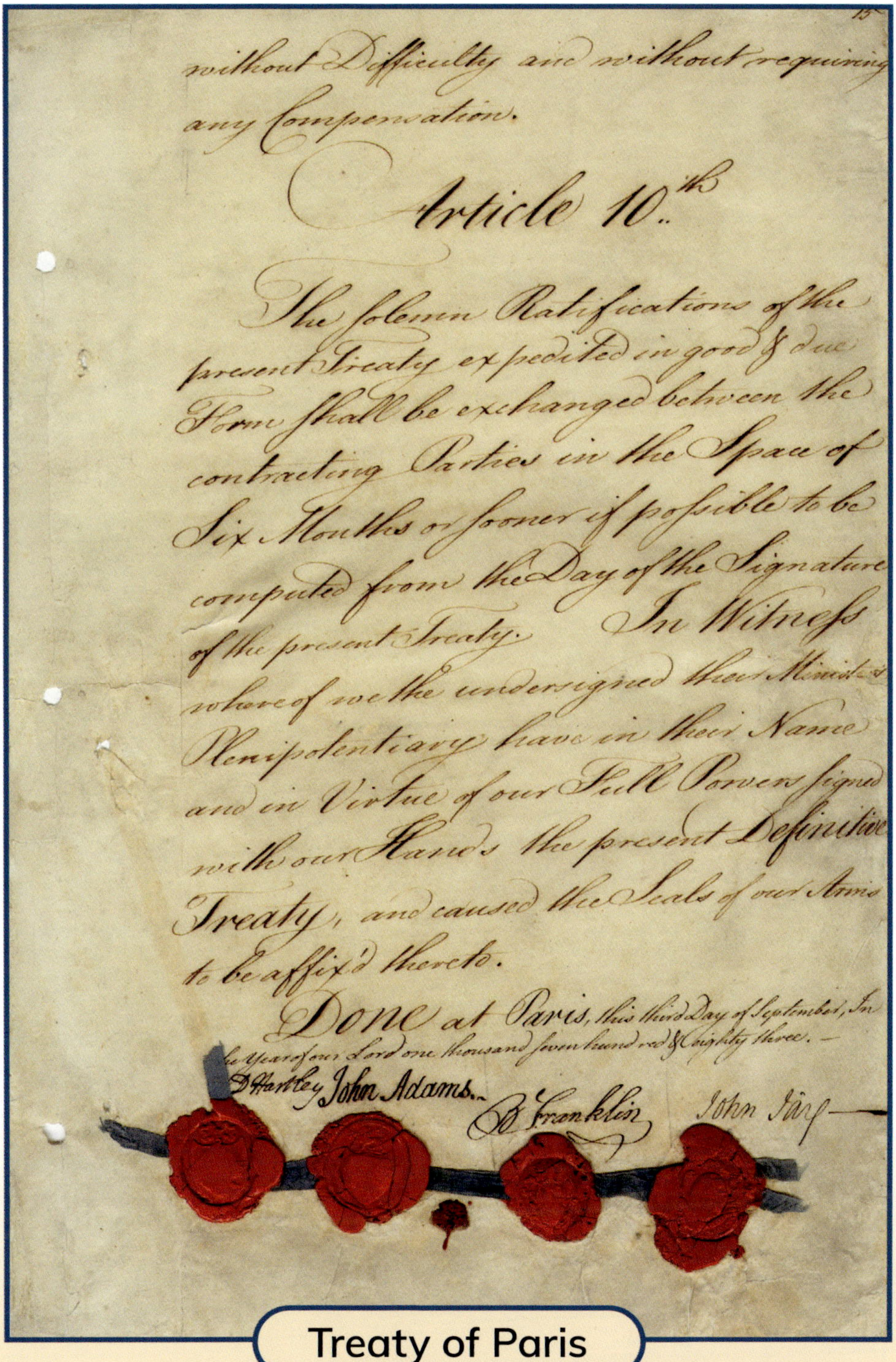
without Difficulty and without requiring any Compensation.

Article 10th.

The solemn Ratifications of the present Treaty expedited in good & due Form shall be exchanged between the contracting Parties in the Space of Six Months or sooner if possible to be computed from the Day of the Signature of the present Treaty. In Witness whereof we the undersigned their Ministers Plenipotentiary have in their Name and in Virtue of our Full Powers signed with our Hands the present Definitive Treaty, and caused the Seals of our Arms to be affix'd thereto.

Done at Paris, this third Day of September, In the Year of our Lord one thousand seven hundred & Eighty three. —

D Hartley John Adams. B Franklin John Jay —

Treaty of Paris

People voting in an election

The Declaration of Independence is still important to all Americans. It means that the government cannot have unfair power over its people. And people have the right to change their government if it is **corrupt** or unfair.

It also means that all Americans are equal. It means that everyone has the right to have a life of freedom and the chance to find happiness.

Women seeking the right to vote

But these ideals have not always been a part of the country's laws and practices. So the words in the Declaration of Independence have challenged the United States over the years too. Americans have fought for the abolition of slavery, for women's right to vote, for civil rights for Black people, and other causes.

Dr. Martin Luther King Jr.

Each generation of Americans has moved the United States closer and closer to living up to the ideals in its Declaration of Independence. They have made the life you live possible. But there's still work to do.

Timeline

June 7, 1776	Richard Lee introduces the idea of independence in Congress.
June 11, 1776	A group is selected to write a declaration of independence.
July 2, 1776	Twelve of the thirteen colonies vote to create a declaration of independence.
July 2–4, 1776	Congress argues about the content of the declaration.
July 4, 1776	Congress approves the Declaration of Independence.
July 8, 1776	The Declaration of Independence is read aloud to the public in Philadelphia for the first time.
August 2, 1776	The Declaration of Independence is signed by about 50 members of Congress.
January 18, 1777	For the first time, the Declaration of Independence is printed with the signers' names.
1800	The original signed copy of the Declaration of Independence moves to Washington, DC.
2003	The Declaration of Indepencence is repaired and restored.
2023	The Declaration of Independence is put on display.

Glossary

adopt (uh-DOPT)—to vote upon and accept as official

boycott (BOY-kot)—to stop buying something to show support for an idea or group of people

colony (KAH-luh-nee)—an area that has been settled by people from another country; a colony is ruled by another country

consent (KUHN-sent)—permission; allowing something to happen

corrupt (kuh-RUPT)—being dishonest or willing to do something that's wrong

declaration (dek-luh-RAY-shuhn)—an important announcement

document (DAHK-yuh-muhnt)—a piece of paper that contains important information

export (ek-SPORT)—to send and sell goods to other countries

parchment (PARCH-muhnt)—a material made from dried and treated animal hide, used to write on

tax (TAKS)—money that people or businesses must give to the government to pay for what the government does

traitor (TRAY-tuhr)—someone who turns against their country

Read More

Bradley, Doug. *20 Things You Didn't Know About the Declaration of Independence.* Buffalo, NY: PowerKids Press, 2024.

Redding, Anna Crowley. *Rescuing the Declaration of Independence: How We Almost Lost the Words That Built America.* New York: HarperCollins, 2020.

Silva, Sadie. *The Declaration of Independence.* New York: Cavendish Square Publishing, 2021.

Internet Sites

Ben's Guide to the U.S. Government: Signing the Declaration of Indendence
bensguide.gpo.gov/j-signing-delaration

Ducksters: American Revolution: The Declaration of Independence
ducksters.com/history/declaration_of_independence.php

National Geographic Kids: Independence Day
kids.nationalgeographic.com/history/article/independence-day

Index

About the Author

Marcia Amidon Lusted has written more than 200 books and 600 articles for young readers of all ages. She also writes and edits for adults and works in sustainable development. Visit www.adventuresin-nonfiction.com for more about her books.